ASHER D

SO SOLID

ASHER D
SO SOLID

JB
JOHN BLAKE

Published by John Blake Publishing Ltd,
3 Bramber Court, 2 Bramber Road,
London W14 9PB, England

First published in hardback in 2004

ISBN 1 904034 96 9

British Library Cataloguing-in-Publication Data:

A catalogue record for this book is available from the British Library.

Design by www.envydesign.co.uk

Printed in Spain by Bookprint

1 3 5 7 9 10 8 6 4 2

Pictures by Geoff Langan

Papers used by John Blake Publishing are natural, recyclable products made from wood grown in sustainable forests. The manufacturing processes conform to the environmental regulations of the country of origin.

contents

Left to right: China, me, Shayon, Natalie and Paniro. My beautiful family.

Prologue

'A SUBSTANTIAL CUSTODIAL SENTENCE ...' The words rang in my brain like alarm bells – they meant I could be going to prison for a very long time.

I'd been waiting nine months since that day when I'd been caught with a loaded gun in my car in London's West End. Nine months of hell – the worst nine months of my life. A time of limbo. I kind of knew I'd be going to jail, but somehow I always had hope – you have to have hope when that sort of thing is hanging over you. But deep down I knew I'd been caught bang to rights, and I was scared – I didn't know what was going to happen to me ...

It had all seemed so different, not so long ago. So Solid Crew, the collective at the centre of my life over the past few years, was riding high. We had a platinum-selling album. '21 Seconds' had entered the chart at number one. Everything I'd worked for and dreamed about since I was old enough to know the direction I'd wanted my life to take was happening just like I wanted.

And now this.

Of course, there was more to the whole thing than met the eye.

'The defendant has pleaded guilty to an extremely serious offence, having in his possession a gun loaded with live ammunition, which in combination was capable of being lethal. The offence is so serious that asubstantial custodial sentence is inevitable.'

Judge Geoffrey Rivlin QC, March 2002

How easy it was for everyone to believe the image that was being portrayed of me as a gun-toting gangster. But the headlines – ASHER D FOUND WITH LOADED GUN – only told half the story. I couldn't help but wonder what people would be saying if the boys who had backed me into a corner where I felt forced to get the gun had had their own way first. Then there might have been a very different tale to tell …

I'm only 21, but I've experienced more ups and downs in my life so far than most people do in an entire lifetime. My story is one of a life on the street. It's not a pretty story, or a fairytale of rags to riches. I want to tell you how it is, for real, without softening the edges or sparing you the gritty details. More than that, I want to open your eyes to what is happening on the street today. I want to tell you how it really is. To do that, I have to go back to one day in June 1982 when a baby was born and his mother named him Ashley Walters …

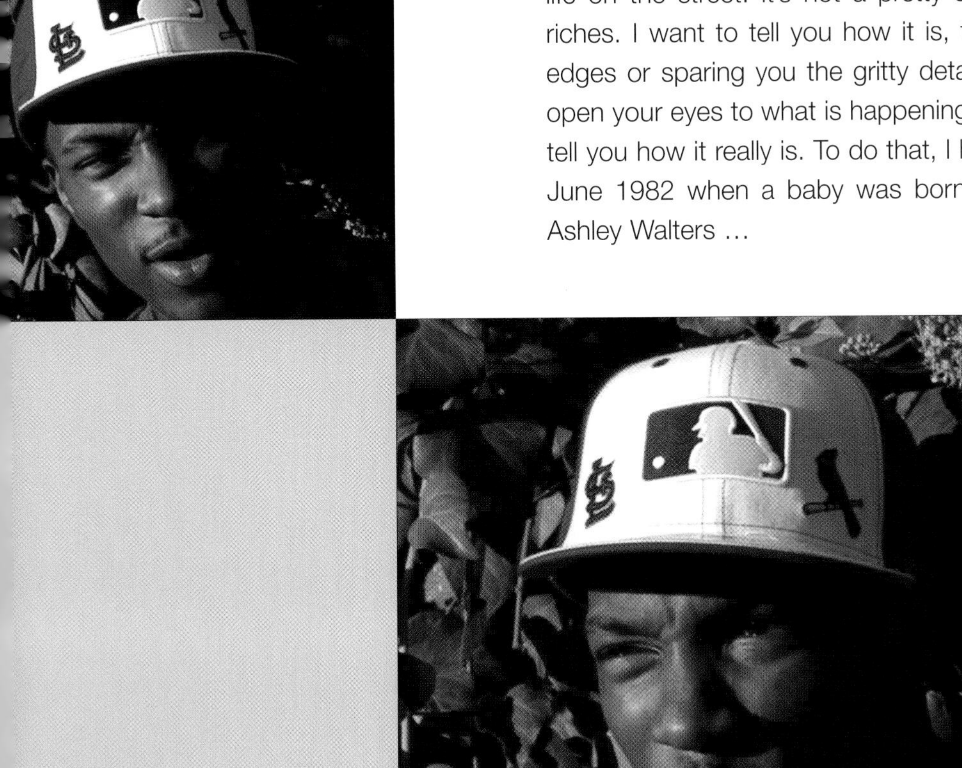

1

Kidnapped!

I COME FROM A BIG FAMILY – A REALLY BIG FAMILY, IN FACT. My mum and my dad aren't together any more, which means that I kind of have two families – one on each side.

I've seven brothers on my dad's side of the family, but I only keep in touch with two of them. Perry, one of my brothers, is 15 now, and we've grown up together, even though we had a different mum. When I was growing up, I never realised how weird the situation was, but Perry's mum and my mum were close friends, and I even used to call Perry's mum 'Mum'! After she and my dad split up I still kept in touch with Perry, and we've become really close over the last few years.

My dad is a waste of space. Don't get me wrong – he's my father and I love him, and nothing will ever change that. But I only see him every now and again, and throughout my life he's never been there for me or any of my brothers. He left my mother just as soon as I was born, and I don't think there's any excuse for that.

I don't think my mum really likes him very much – who can blame

Me on the North Peckham Estate,
near where I grew up.

her after what he did? – but to her credit she's never stopped me from seeing him. She's always thought that he should be a part of my life, that a little boy needs his dad, and because of that she's always encouraged me to spend time with him. And so it's thanks to her, I suppose, that me and Dad have never become strangers. Even so, whenever I went to see him, I'd never actually spend all that much time with him.

Dad really hasn't done much with his life. He claims to be a painter and decorator, but he's never had a steady job and he hardly makes any money at all. I don't worry that he'll read this and what I've said will come as a surprise, because he knows exactly how I feel about him. Obviously, when I was younger, I didn't know how to voice my opinion about this kind of stuff, but now that I'm older it's all different. It's strange, because the relationship that we have is not like a father-and-son relationship. It's more like we're just friends. If I'm honest, I'd have to say that

the relationship changed a bit when I became famous. It's not exactly that Dad became jealous, but I think he started to feel that his son couldn't look up to him any more so he'd kind of have to look up to his son.

It's funny how fame can sometimes affect other people ...

But, despite everything, this is my dad we're talking about, and I love him. He'll be my dad till the day he dies, and I'll always be there to take care of him. But sometimes I don't think he understands how I feel – he seems to me like he feels he has to impress me, always telling me a load of exaggerated stuff about how well business is going just to make himself look better in my eyes. All that stuff hurts me – I just want him to tell me how it really is. I just want him to keep it real.

My mum is very, very different. She lives in Borough and works as Head of Personnel for a company. She's always worked – I've honestly never known her not work – and she's made her way to the top of the ladder. I like to think that her motivation and determination to do things has rubbed off on me.

We've got the same personality, my mum and me – I'm exactly like her. If you met her, you'd know we were just the same. In fact, you'd probably think she was my sister – she looks young, in fact she is young, just 36 now.

When I was growing up, I lived with my mum in Southampton Way, Peckham. It's right opposite the North Peckham Estate where most of the drug dealing and whatever takes place. I grew up right in the middle of all that. My primary school was just

'I used to get robbed on my way to primary school – just for my dinner money or whatever else I happened to have on me. It was no big deal – just a thing that used to happen to people.'

round the corner. It was a good school, I liked it, but I haven't really kept in touch with any friends from that place. I used to get robbed on my way to primary school – just for my dinner money or whatever else I happened to have on me. At the time I must have been eight or nine years old, and the kids who were doing it to me were maybe 15. It was no big deal – just a thing that used to happen to people. You had to be careful which way round you walked to school, otherwise you'd walk straight into their hands …

I was a bit of a ruffian when I was younger, always having fights around the area where I lived. It's not because there wasn't any discipline at home – when I was little I was scared of my mum. She never hit me, but she'd give me that serious look on her face, and I knew from the tone of her voice – don't muck around! In my mind, I always wanted to please my mum, so I never crossed her directly. I'd never be one of those kids who'd play truant; you'd always find me in school. OK, I might not have been doing the work! I might have been sleeping on the table! But I made sure I was always there.

Being at school was just a façade, though. I made it look like I was doing everything right, getting my work done, but, after school, I was out there, man!

I fell in with a gang. You know how it is when you get a whole load of kids from one estate or one area, and they all fall in with their own crew. I became part of that scene, because that's just what you do, what you follow. These people were doing all sorts of things – drugs, stealing cars, robbing. I was only nine or ten at the time, but I was hanging out with guys who were 15, 16, 17. But I was always a follower, never at the forefront – I suppose it was because I didn't really want to do what I was doing. I didn't want to get stabbed, I didn't want to get shot at.

There used to be this place in Peckham where the older brother of a friend called Mark – who used to live on the Peckham Estate – once took us. You'd pull up a drain panel and climb down the tunnel and there was this whole other world down there. I don't know exactly what it was – a sewer or something – but it had all these lights hooked up and it would always be full of kids, all sitting on pipes and smoking cigarettes, weed, crack even, all out of the view of the public, and more importantly the police. To this day I can't remember where it is – I only went there once – but I do still wonder if it's still there. It probably is.

We used to do loads of weird shit like that – clambering round building sites, getting stuck, climbing walls, breaking your legs, whatever. That was just our life, being rough. And let me tell you that, as a kid, I saw some mad stuff. Sometimes, because I was so young, I didn't realise how mad it was. One day I was playing on my bike in the middle of the estate and this black boy comes out and he's clearly got something in his pocket. At the time, I didn't know it was a gun, I just knew he had something in his pocket and he kept his hand on it. He was a bit in the distance, but I watched him anyway. He started having a conversation with somebody else, and things started to get a bit heated …

I didn't actually see him get shot, but I heard the gun go off and when I looked again this guy is lying on the floor and there are people running over to see what happened. Like I said, I was just a kid, so I didn't know what was happening, and at the time I don't think it really affected me. I didn't understand about guns, and I've no idea if the guy died or not. But those experiences affect me now that I understand what they were all about, and they've made me paranoid about all sorts of things.

Back in the day, as I got older, I'd get myself into situations, bad situations when I think about them now, like the time I was kidnapped. That's what the police would call it, but coming from the street it was just a fact of life – a couple of guys will see you on the street and say, 'Hey, you're coming with us.' And they'll take you with them while they go and rob someone.

When it happened to me I must have been about 13 years old. I got off the bus and started walking down the road, and these two boys see me. They had familiar faces, I'd seen them around before, and I just knew something was going to happen. I couldn't run because I knew they had me in their sights. They come up to me, all casually, and say, 'Hey, do you want to make some money?'

'Yeah, of course I want to make some money.' But all the time I'm thinking, Only if it's something easy.

'Well, you've got to get on the bus with us,' says one of the two guys.

'What do you mean, get on the bus?' But I knew completely what they meant, and I also knew that if I tried to run they'd just catch me. I had a bus pass, but one of the boys had the cheek to take it from me and leave me without one. I started thinking, I should run now, make some noise, but at the end of the day it came down to a question of pride. I guess I just didn't want to feel embarrassed, so I went with them …

They had me for a whole day. First they took me to some girls' house, and the girls were going mad at them: 'Let him go, let him go home!' But the boys just laughed. They clearly had no intention of letting me go anywhere.

So then they took me to some place and told me that they wanted me to snatch an old lady's bag. They said that they'd find the victim, and I was to go and rob her, run back to the estate and wait for them, and we'd all split the money. At that point, I just thought, Fuck it, and I ran and ran as fast as my legs would carry me. The boys gave chase, picking up stones as they did so to throw at me. But I just kept on running – thankfully they couldn't catch up with me – until I got home.

By this stage in my life, my mum had twigged that I'd started getting a bit bad. I'd been coming home late from school and getting into all kinds of trouble, and so, when I told her what had happened, she didn't believe me. 'Stop chatting shit!' she said. 'You know you've just been out doing something, smoking or whatever.' I had to persuade her that, no, this really had happened, and so she said, 'OK, let's call the police.' The police came to the house and I had to make a statement. But even though I knew who the boys were – and I still know – I kept quiet. One of the first rules of the street is don't be a grass. I could've given their names at any time, but I didn't – Asher D's no G. To this day I still see them, but now they have to look up to me. The roles have been reversed.

That was the first time I remember having any contact with the police. It was not to be the last ...

2

The Stabbing

AS I GREW UP, I LIVED A KIND OF A DOUBLE LIFE. On the one hand, I was getting involved with the gangs around the Peckham Estate – rough stuff that was really teaching me about life on the street. At the same time the seeds were being sown that would lead me to becoming a performing artist.

I went to the Sylvia Young stage school from the age of five or six. It was Mum's idea – she's pushy, and she was making sure that I developed the same kind of drive that she has. It was like I had two lives, because when you go to those classes – Saturday classes – you've got to behave! I learned all sorts of stuff there, even ballet, but at the time it wasn't really my thing. I just did it to keep my mum happy. Still, it was fun, even if I didn't know then that it was what I wanted to do, and so I stayed with the Sylvia Young Agency when I left.

I started getting bits and pieces of work – adverts and the like – and then people began to realise that I had a good voice for radio. And so I started doing radio drama, just little kids' plays, which led to me getting theatre work.

My first stage appearance was in a play called *Children of Eden* at the Prince Edward Theatre. I played the part of Abel, but I ended up getting the sack when the show started running out of money and they had to get rid of some of the artists. It ended up that the guy who was originally playing a dog got to play my part as well!

I went on to perform in *Carmen Jones* at the Old Vic in Waterloo, followed by more adverts and then I did a run in *Oliver!* at the Palladium. This led to some offers to do low-budget films, and on the back of those I was offered a good movie role in a film called *Storm Damage*. That part took my acting career on to a whole new level and gave me a lot of respect from casting directors and other people in the industry. I'm still getting work off the back of that role even now. I was beginning to get a taste of fame, and gradually it became clear to me that performing was what I wanted to do with my life. And my love of performing wasn't just confined to acting.

A lot of artists, when you ask them about their musical influences as they were growing up will say, 'Yeah, my parents listened to this or that.' But I grew up with my mum, and she didn't really listen to music, it wasn't something that was important in her life. Oh, she had a few Aretha Franklin records, but she never had any mad music collection – maybe five or six records at the most. As for my dad, I never really lived with him, so I don't much know what kind of music he was into.

In fact, as I got older, I probably influenced my mum's taste in music rather than the other way round. Now she listens to basically the same kind of music that I do. She doesn't listen to the music that I make, but we've got the same kind of taste – neo-soul, R 'n' B, jazz – and I think I probably gave her that taste (although I'm sure she'd argue that point!)

So I wasn't surrounded by music at home, but socially I was always surrounded by music. I had friends who were deep into rap and garage, and you know how it is: when your friends are doing it, you kind of go along with it. Also, I was always involved in the

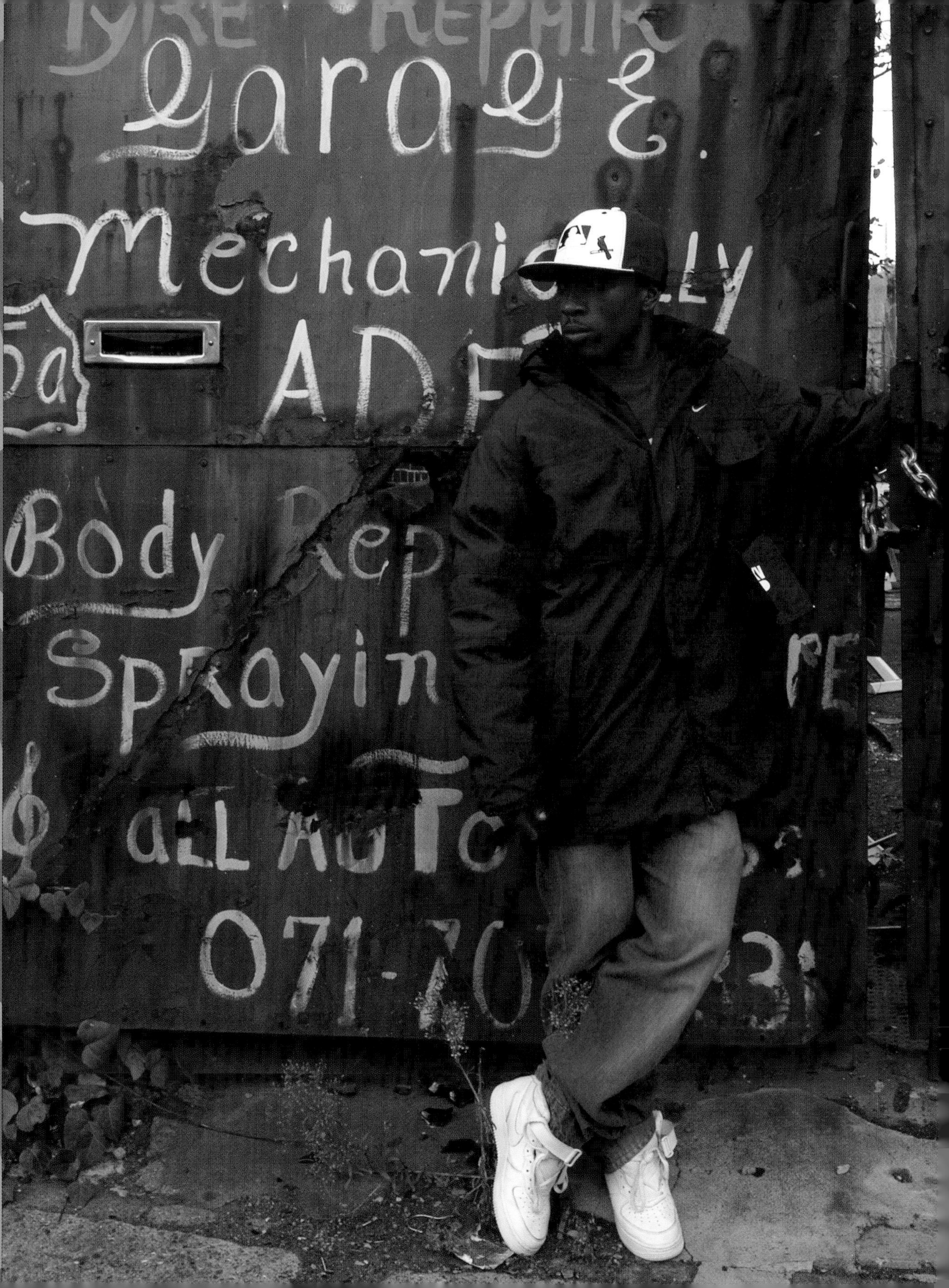
Garage
Body Rep
Sprayin
ALL AUTO
071-70

music side of my acting – *Oliver!* and stuff. It's not the same sort of music by a long shot, but it's all about rhythm, and it gave me a push into the entertainment side of things.

I really got into music in a big way when the jungle and drum 'n' bass thing came along – the real hard stuff. That was the garage of the time, the rap of the time. On the streets, that was it – you'd go to clubs and it was all jungle music. I remember a series of CDs called *Junglemania* – my mum used to buy them for me for Christmas.

At that time, garage music was already around, but it was more of a house/techno thing, and we saw that as white boys' music, not ours. But as garage music started to develop a bit more, and as more people jumped on the bandwagon, the beat started to change a bit, started to gel with the R 'n' B thing as more hip-hop samples and drumbeats crept in. That's when the rappers on the street started to get on to it and they took it to a whole other extreme, gave it that urban feel. People like MC Creed, PSG and Pied Piper were responsible for developing the urban garage sound we have today. It was still kind of commercial, but it was more underground than it was before, so people latched on to it. It was something that black musicians didn't really create; rather we took what already existed and made something out of it.

From that moment, everyone wanted to be an MC or a producer, and I was no exception. I got involved in MCing through going to a youth club – St Andrew's Youth Club in Victoria. We used to go there after school for a couple of hours, and they had their own decks. DJs would bring their own records, there'd be a mike there and we'd go down and MC with each other – battle it out at the mike, trying to see who's best, like in the movie *8 Mile*.

I didn't really want to do it at first. I just went along and thought to myself, Yeah, I could do that if I wanted to, if I went home and practised. That's the kind of guy I was. I wouldn't shoot my mouth off and say, 'Yeah, you lot, I'm gonna start MCing!' I just listened to them doing it and thought, Fuck it, let me see if I can do that. So I went home, wrote a couple of lyrics on the sly and practised it to myself. Then one day, at the youth club, I said, 'Yeah, OK, I'll give it a go,' got up in front of everyone and just did it. I didn't do it for long – I must have had two lyrics of 16 bars each – but I got applauded for it and if felt good. I liked the buzz of it, and it all went from there.

After that I went along twice a week, getting up in front of the crowd each evening. There'd be girls there, of course, and they'd be cheering me on – or cheering the other guy on. But a lot of times I won the contest, not because, I think, my lyrics were particularly good at that time, but I was a popular guy in school and had a lot of people following me, a lot of support. I suppose the truth is that people knew that, if they didn't support Ashley tonight, they ain't gonna have no friends at school tomorrow … I won it like that, and that's really where the love of performing the music came.

But if I was growing more popular with my peers through my MCing, it didn't mean that the streets of south London were becoming any less dangerous a place for me. After the incident when the two boys kidnapped me, I found that it felt a bit weird being out, seeing people. I found that I began to develop a fear of what was going to happen to me if I got myself into certain situations. But at the same time I was young and hot-headed, and

'It just felt like a punch, so I took the blow and carried on fighting. I didn't know what was going on, so as I was fighting this guy, I was bleeding more and more and ripping the wound open even further. I couldn't feel anything, though, so I just carried on.'

so I suppose it was inevitable that I was going to encounter dangerous people and dangerous times …

Soon after I started MCing at the youth club, something happened to the young Ashley Walters that nearly brought his career to a very abrupt and messy end. It was a weekday evening, and I remember it was dark outside so we must have stayed behind at school – we used to meet up with girls after school and smoke weed or whatever. It must have been about 5.30 or 6.00 pm. We started making our way to the youth club, and on the way we passed an off-licence. Three of my friends decided that they wanted to buy some alcohol, so they went into the shop. At the same time, two white guys went in to buy some drink or whatever. What happened inside the shop, I don't know, because we were all standing outside, but after a while one of my friends came out and he was arguing with one of the white guys. They weren't English, I don't think – maybe Portuguese – but they were big, strapping lads, not the kind of guys to mess with.

At the time, I was the biggest out of all my friends – they were all real midgets! – so I go up to them, all hot-headed: 'What's going on?' I pushed my friend out of the way and, from that moment on, it was my argument.

So I'm arguing with the guy, and suddenly, out of nowhere, he punches me and I'm down. My friends pile in, but they're so small and this guy is so big he just throws them off. At this point the other white guy, who must have been finishing off paying for whatever he was buying, walks out of the shop and sees what's happening. He grabs a bottle, smashes it on the kerb, comes up to me and stabs me right in the neck.

It just felt like a punch, so I took the blow and carried on fighting. I didn't know what was going on, so as I was fighting this guy, I was bleeding more and more and ripping the wound open even further. I couldn't feel anything, though, so I just carried on.

Eventually the white boys ran off – this guy came out of the chip shop, saw that I was bleeding and scared them off. And that's when I realised I'd been cut. I felt my neck and thought, What's all this wet stuff? Then I felt the skin flapping in the wind, realised what had happened and just wanted to faint – seriously, it was disgusting. It felt like somebody had poured a bucket of water over my head. One of my friends even started crying when he saw it.

I took my jumper off and wrapped it round my neck while we tried to find a phone box. I'm thinking, I'm dying here, and all my friends were standing around crying! Luckily, a police car was patrolling and as it drove by the police saw what was happening. They get out of the car, walk up to us – and start questioning us for five or ten minutes! I'm saying, 'Are you taking the piss.' And one of my friends says to them, 'Look, he's dying, can you take him to the hospital, please?'

'No,' they say, 'you have to wait for the ambulance. We can't take you.' All the time I'm losing mad amounts of blood, but they can't take me – it's the law. Soon enough, I blacked out, and when I woke up I was in hospital. I was there for two days, and nearly had to have a blood transfusion I lost that much blood.

It took me a long time to dare to leave the house after that little episode. But, as I was beginning to learn, acts of violence like that were part and parcel of life on the street …

3

IT WAS AROUND THE TIME OF THE STABBING THAT I FIRST MET NATALIE, WHO IS STILL MY GIRLFRIEND AND THE MOTHER OF MY CHILDREN. I met her in school when she was going out with my best friend. They broke up, not because of me, after about two years of being together; one thing led to another and we got it together. It wasn't much of a relationship at first, but then she fell pregnant.

I was scared. My initial reaction was not to tell anyone – not even my mum. But, of course, I couldn't do that. I realised I had to bite the bullet so I thought to myself, OK, Ashley, let's get it over with. I went over to the house, told my mum and she just couldn't believe it. She was so upset.

As I looked at her crying, something clicked in my mind. All of a sudden it became clear to me that this was a turning point: it was the moment that I realised I had to make something of my life. I was going to have to find a way to earn a living, decently and legitimately, so that I could take care of the responsibilities that were coming towards me. And the way that I'd been hustling a few bucks up till that point was going to have to stop …

When I was young, I used to see these guys who had everything – the flash cars, the jewellery, the big houses – and I used to think to myself, How did they get that? At the time, I had no idea. Then, when I was old enough, someone told me. It was crack.

That was the world I was surrounded by as I grew up, so I suppose it was inevitable that, sooner or later, I'd find myself embroiled in the drug scene. I first started selling weed when I was about 16. That was how I made my money – that and a bit of acting. You'd buy the gear on consignment, sell it off and then pay back your supplier. So say you buy a couple of ounces at £80 an ounce, that's £160. You could make about £240 selling that off, which means you'd pay the £160 back to your supplier and keep about £80.

Trouble was, I was just about the worst drug dealer in London! I just wasn't doing it right and financially speaking I was losing more from doing it than I was gaining. I was overspending, had too many expenses and above all I just wasn't selling it on quickly enough – if you don't sell it in a certain amount of time it dries out. I ended up

SO SOLID

being stuck with dried-out weed which I couldn't make any money from, but of course I still had to pay back the person I'd bought it from, so I ended up in debt.

After a while I just thought, I'm wasting my time here. And, looking back, I can see that the fact that I was such a useless dealer was really a good thing. I didn't want to be a dealer, I didn't want to be in that position, and I didn't want to be going to jail. But I was doing what I was doing to get myself out of a certain situation, and that's just what everyone who gets involved in the drug scene is doing to start off with. Everyone's looking for a way out, and that's why they get involved in stuff like crack. But, dealing crack, the way I see it is there's only three ways you can end up: dead, in jail or on it yourself. There was this white boy who I knew who lived in Camberwell, and he made mad money. He always had new cars, money in his pocket, girls, everything. But then he got on it himself, and once that happens there's no looking back …

I can see how people get attracted to crack. You could be broke today, sell some crack and be a rich man next week. The mark-up is unbelievable, and I can tell you now that there were plenty of times that I thought of going down that route. I know people who have made a million pounds out of it – they just save their money and, when it reaches a certain level, they stop. But then there are people who do it because they like the idea of the gangster lifestyle, and that's when it starts to get real scary. Crack deals are dangerous, man, and, with every crack deal that happens, the street becomes a more dangerous place.

You could be broke today, sell some crack, and be a rich man next week. The mark-up is unbelievable, and I can tell you now that there were plenty of times that I thought of going down that route. I know people who have made a million pounds out of it …

Crack is the most addictive drug there is, and I don't care what anyone says – not the media or the government who are all trying to make it sound like it's a problem confined to south London – it's everywhere. The drugs are feeding everything, they're the cause of all the dangerous crime out on the streets. The guys who are getting shot are all involved with dangerous people – it's not law-abiding citizens who are walking down the street getting shot, it's people involved in drugs. All the killings and shooting you hear about, it's the crackheads, people taking drugs to get high and get the courage to go out and shoot someone. Give a crackhead a gun and say, 'Go shoot that person and I'll give you crack,' and they'll do it, man. They don't care what they do or who sees them. I've seen them rolling cigarettes with crack in them in the street, in full view of everyone. The cats sell them a rock and they're rolling it, right there.

So, when I knew I was going to be a father, I could see that, unless I made something positive of my life, I was looking at going down a very, very dangerous road.

I was lucky. I had something else in my life to stop me going down that route – music. Through MCing down at the youth club, I became friendly with other people in my area who were into the same thing. I've only got two real close friends who I've known for ever: Michael (who we call Mouse because he was so small when he was at school) and Dooz (people call him that because no one can pronounce his real name). Anyway, Mouse had a set of friends in his part of Camberwell and a couple of them were DJs. One of them was called Big Kid and he was in a crew called Living Legend which originally consisted of him, Neutrino (later part of Oxide and Neutrino) and another guy called Billy the Kid. They worked on a pirate radio station called Supreme FM.

A pirate radio station is basically an illegal radio station. Some clever brainbox has worked out a way to nab a frequency and get their station on air. I don't know who worked it out, or when it started, but pirate radio stations have been around for a long while

In my bedroom with my friends
Mouse and Dooz.

KEVIN LYTTLE
SPECIAL COLLECTOR'S EDITION
ATTRACTION

now. They're often just run out of some flat somewhere – and, believe me, I've seen stations run out of some pretty disgusting flats before now, with pigeons and shit and squatters. Some people just do it in their own house – just a normal house and you go through and there's a room with a radio transmitter in it. These days a lot of them are run out of warehouses – people rent out warehouse rooms because I suppose they must feel more secure there, as pirate radios are being raided a lot of the time by the Department of Trade and Industry.

Like I say, I met Big Kid and Living Legend through Mouse, and I went up to Supreme FM with them. I'd made a tape of myself MCing – just a demo kind of thing so people could hear what I was doing – to give to the manager of the station. The manager ran the station out of his flat in Brixton. When I got there, I gave him the demo and he didn't even listen to it! He just said, 'Yeah, come on the station, when do you want to start?' I swear I went on that same night.

After that, I was just there all the time, 24/7. It drove my mum nuts – she never knew where the hell I was. The radio was always broadcasting, and we'd be on it from noon to five the next morning, stop for a couple of hours, then come back on. We were swept away by the eagerness of it all, by the buzz of just having a voice. At the time, Supreme was the biggest pirate radio in south London. We knew there were a lot of listeners because once a month we'd put on our own raves. They'd only be advertised on Supreme, and when you got to the rave it would be sold out – ram jam. So we knew that we had to have several thousand listeners.

I arrived at Supreme FM as Ashley Walters, and everyone called me Asher – that was it, just Asher. But a lot of people ask me how I got the name Asher D, and it was around this time that it happened.

There was another guy on another station also called Asher. He was well known at the time and he rang up the manager of Supreme saying, 'You can't have this kid calling himself Asher as well.'

So the manager comes to me and says, 'You can't call yourself Asher. Either you change your name to something else, or you can't be on the station.'

'What am I supposed to call myself?' Asher was, after all, my name, and I didn't want to change it. That's who I am, that's what all my friends call me and everything.

'Well, put something on the end,' he told me. 'A "P" or a "B" or something.'

I went through the whole alphabet. 'Asher A, Asher B, Asher C …' Eventually I decided on Asher D – somehow it just sounded right, and that was that. Asher D was born.

So on the one hand I was hustling a living trying to sell a bit of weed, desperately trying not to be seduced into the path of dealing in crack. On the other hand I'd found an outlet for my creativity, a platform on which to perform. My life could truly have gone either way. But then, at Supreme FM, I met someone who was to have an enormous effect on my life. He was the main MC of his own crew. He called himself Megaman, and he was leader of the So Solid Crew.

4

Megaman and Me

I'D LISTENED TO SUPREME FM EVEN BEFORE LIVING LEGEND TOOK ME UP THERE AND I STARTED BEING A PART OF IT, SO I KNEW ABOUT THE CREW THAT CALLED THEMSELVES SO SOLID. They used to MC on Supreme, and I would listen to their lyrics and try and write the same as them, to get inspiration from what they were doing. So when I arrived at Supreme, I knew they'd be there, and I knew what to expect.

I'm the kind of guy who, if I don't know how to do something, I'll go home and practise it till I can. It was like that with So Solid – I used to sit and watch them, go home, practise and come back being able to do what they did. That's how it works, when you look up to someone, when you look to them for inspiration.

At the beginning, in those early days at Supreme, the crew was not nearly so big as it is now. At that time I only saw G Man, who wasn't involved musically but was involved business-wise – organising raves and what have you; then there was Mega, the main MC, then Mac, DJ Dan the Man and DJ PDS on the decks,

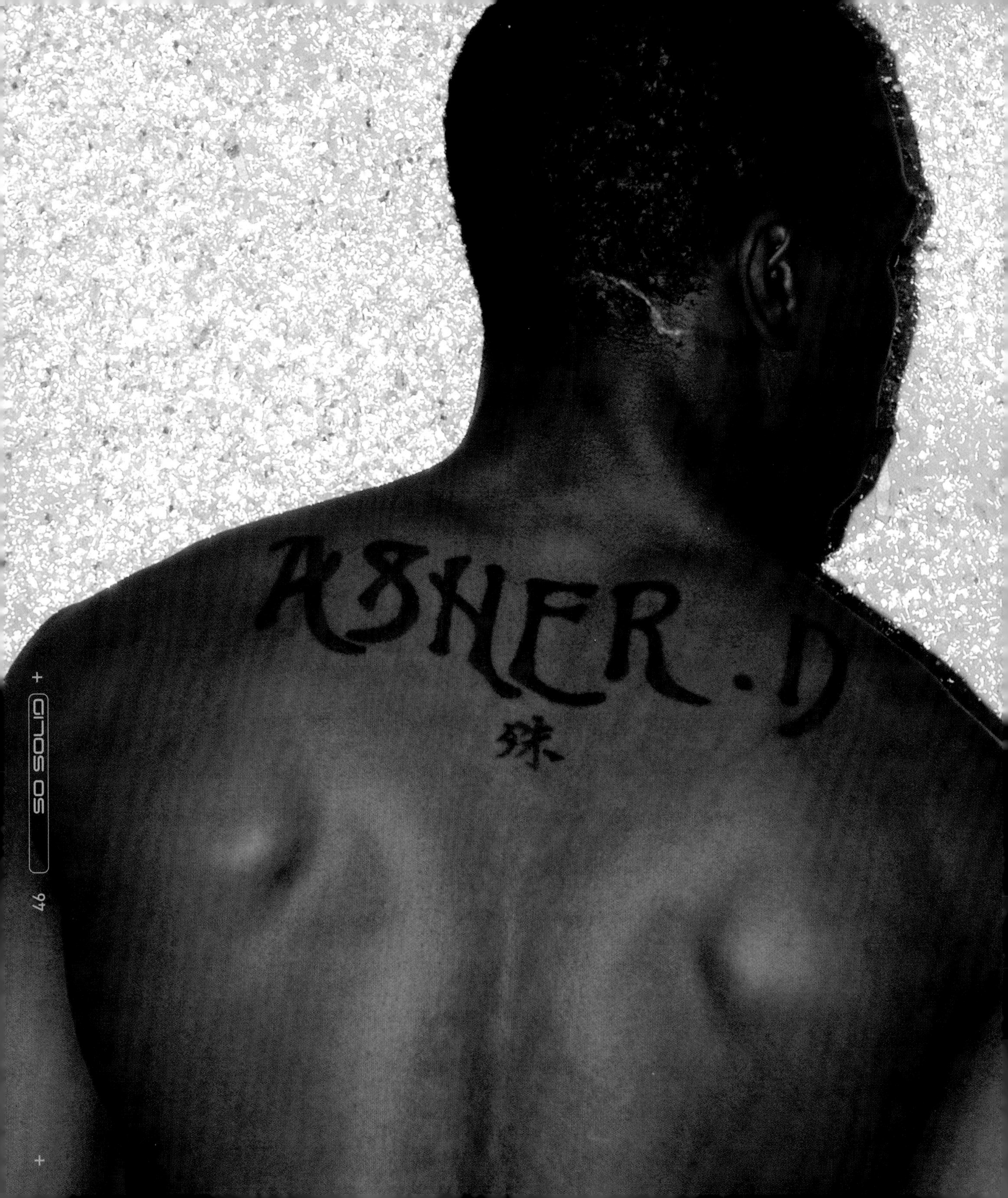

and Romeo. Five of them, basically, doing the music thing, and then G Man on the underground side of it.

The time came when So Solid and Supreme decided it was time to part company. The crew decided that the moment had come for them to start up their own thing, their own station, so they moved back to the area around Battersea and Mega, who had a lot of contacts on the music side of things, called up everyone he knew and said, 'Do you want to come with us or stay with Supreme?'

He rang me and said the same thing, and I didn't even have to think about it. 'I'm coming with you guys!' I was really happy to hear him ask me that, because at the time I wasn't really sure if they knew who I was, what I was doing – I'd never really talked to them much and I certainly didn't know that Mega had been listening to my thing. So when he called me I remember thinking, Well, if they're asking me to go with them, they must think I've got something, some sort of potential, so I was gone like a shot.

So it was then that Delight FM was born, and I started MCing on the new station. At the time, though, I still wasn't part of So Solid Crew. I was freelance, without my own DJ or anything, so it became natural that I'd get up and MC with Mega or whoever. It sort of became second nature. Then, one day, I was in the Delight studios – the station was running out of some girl's flat at the time – and we were just sitting around in the living room while someone else was doing their two-hour set. Out of the blue, Mega said, 'Do you want to be in So Solid?'

I just looked at him, so he repeated himself. 'Do you want to be in the Crew?'

'What do you mean, do I want to be in the Crew? Of course I want to be in the Crew!'

'Well, OK then,' Mega told me. 'You're in the Crew.' And he started telling me how much he was into my lyrics, that he would listen to me when he was driving, all that kind of stuff.

It was one of the best moments in my life. I'd gone from listening

to these guys on the radio to becoming one of them. Everything seemed to fall into place that moment when Mega took me under his wing. So Solid is like a family, and Mega's the father figure: he'll bring you in, look after you for a bit and then move on to find the next member of the family.

So I had my acting, and now I was a fully fledged member of the So Solid Crew. Things were heading in the right direction for me, but, when Natalie became pregnant, I knew that things had to step up a gear, that I had to really work at my career in order to make a real name for myself. At this point, remember, So Solid weren't making a whole load of money. We didn't have a record deal, and we weren't well known outside of the fan base of Delight FM and Supreme. Fortunately for me – fortunately for all of us – we didn't have to wait long.

So Solid Crew's record deal came about thanks to the success of Oxide and Neutrino. Oxide used to be with Supreme – just as a freelance DJ who would turn up with his brother and do his own thing – and Neutrino was part of Living Legend, the crew that had taken me along to Supreme in the first place. When we made the move to Delight FM, Mega called them both and they came with us and, once we got to the new station, they just gelled. They started working together a lot, and eventually Neutrino left Living Legend and joined up with Oxide.

Soon enough, they were starting to pay for their own studio time so that they could go into the studio and work on beats for themselves. After a while they made this particular beat together and,

The day '21 Seconds' went to
number 1, we were touring, promoting
the single up and down the country.
I remember we were in the car,
listening to the Radio 1 chart countdown and when we heard we were
number 1 we just went mad!
SO SOLID
67

At The Dairy, the studio where I record.

every time we'd do a set on the radio, we'd play this beat. And the record label tuned in. It was East West Records who listened to the tune, liked what they heard and got in contact.

Because of Oxide and Neutrino's success, we became inspired to do the same as them, to start working on our own beats just like they had. We knew we had our own promotion outlet, through our radio station, and Oxide and Neutrino were supporting us just like we were supporting them. That's the So Solid ethos – everyone helps each other and we all share in each other's success. Mega and Romeo made a tune called 'Oh No', and we started playing that on the radio; and then, through Oxide and Neutrino, we met somebody who was to play an incredibly important role in the success of So Solid Crew, and in my life in particular: manager Albert Samuel.

Albert started helping us and, as if from nowhere, we've got a deal for 'Oh No'. Boom. Signed. Just like that. And that was the beginning of it all. Thanks to Albert we got our next single deal, an album deal and from there it just grew ...

'Oh No' did OK, but the problem we had with it was that it had six mixes of the same song on the single. As soon as you put six tracks on a disc, it's classed officially as an album, so its sales were listed on the album chart, not the singles chart. With the amount of sales it notched up, though, if it had gone into the singles charts it would have been number 3, which is pretty cool. So, even though we didn't really make that much of an impact with 'Oh No', we knew we had it in us, and it gave us a real impetus to work hard on the next single. It was called '21 Seconds'.

That was when the buzz really started to happen. Everyone was saying, 'Hey, it's the same guys that did "Oh No",' and, thanks to that, the single went straight in at number one.

All of a sudden, the fame that I'd been trying to get through my acting since I was four or five years old came at me in two weeks. I remember just being in a daze thinking, Wow, this is heavy shit. I still didn't have any money, so it wasn't like I was rich or anything, but all of a sudden I was getting recognised wherever I went.

The day '21 Seconds' went to number one, we were touring, promoting the single up and down the country. I remember we were in the car, listening to the Radio 1 chart countdown and when we heard we were number one we just went mad! That night, a big party was thrown for us at some bar – I can't remember where – and we all just got slaughtered! My girlfriend was there, everyone was nicely drunk and it was just the best feeling ever. We'd all achieved something we all always wanted.

Suddenly I was getting all this publicity, I was up there on the video, and I knew that my solo career could take off from here. I knew that this was what I needed to get me out of the slump I was in. But even though I had the hype around me, and all the excitement, I still didn't have much money. There were 35 of us in the Crew and, once you start splitting the money, you're left with almost nothing. So even in those days I was still surviving, still selling a bit of weed on the side – I had to carry on doing that until about the time that the album came out. But, by the time Shayon was born, we'd signed the first album and I knew things were going to go well for me. It's funny, if Natalie hadn't got pregnant, I don't think I'd have had the impetus to really make it. That was the crucial moment, the moment when I knew that this could no longer be a hobby, it had to be a career. And what a crazy career it turned out to be.

Fame is a funny thing. Once you achieve it, you realise that it's sometimes not what you imagined it would be. Don't get me wrong – it's great – but, even if you yourself remain unaffected by it, you never know what your own fame is going to do to the people around you.

All of a sudden I found that the way my friends were with me changed, and for the worse. I don't know why. I couldn't tell if it's because they're jealous or not, because they just distanced themselves from me. It doesn't really bother me that much because, if they're gone now, it means they weren't really my friends in the beginning. I've got two good friends – Dooz and Mouse – and that's kind of all I need. They keep me focused, keep my feet on the ground. When I go out with them there's no question of me having to pay for everything, and they do that to make a point – our friendship is nothing to do with money. We're equal, I'm no bigger than they are.

Nowadays, I don't try and find new friends, because I never know if people want to get involved with me for reasons of their own. Before it was simple: I didn't have any money, I didn't have any fame, I couldn't give anyone anything, so there was no reason for people to want to get to know me for any ulterior motive. Now I find I can't really trust anyone. I think that that is why you often see artists getting together with other artists – because they can't find anyone else who understands the situation they're in.

Natalie finds it a very difficult situation to handle. She has done from day one. She puts up with it, but it's always been a problem for her. When she went into labour with our daughter, I was in the middle of filming. I rushed home to pick her up, took her to the hospital and she had the baby in about an hour – it was real quick. But then they were waiting for me on set. I had to rush back and leave her there in the hospital. I didn't even have the opportunity to hold my child. I know that stuff like that is very hurtful for her, very hard for her to deal with.

The problem is that all these things are part and parcel of being famous. With the success of '21 Seconds' So Solid Crew were one of the biggest, most talked-about groups in the industry. But I was soon to discover that being famous was to have very much more sinister repercussions; and I was soon to move from being famous to being infamous …

5

The Gun

SO SOLID HAD MADE IT. Everyone had heard of us, Asher D was on his way to becoming a household name, and I couldn't go anywhere without being surrounded by fans. All the cars I had had to be tinted out so I could drive around without being recognised. I couldn't just walk into a shop like a regular person, and I'd never get out of my car or come out of my house at 3.30 in the afternoon because that's when everyone was coming home from school. If I passed the bus stop, I'd get rushed by fans.

It became crazy. My friend's girlfriend is a singer, and Swiss and I started a management company to try to manage her. She was playing at a talent show one night, so me and a few people wanted to go down and see her. On purpose we got there a bit late so that the lights were dark inside the auditorium when we arrived, and I went in the back entrance so no one could see me arrive. As the show came to a close, I said, 'Let's slip out ten minutes before the end so no one sees us.'

But nobody wanted to. They were all saying, 'It'll be fine, we'll just go out the back when it's finished. No one will notice us.' So sure enough we stayed, and as the lights went up everyone sees my face and that was it – rush! The audience was all girls, aged 14 to 18, and about 150 of them chased us to the car, crying, trying to kiss us and hug us while my friends were trying to push them back so we could actually get inside the car. It was nuts. Obviously I love all that stuff – it's great – but it can sometimes get you down when you just want to go somewhere quietly and you can't.

On the up side, I found I could start living the life I'd been looking forward to leading, and part of that meant meeting famous people who really inspired me. Just after '21 Seconds' went to number one, we got the call asking us to support Eminem at the Docklands Arena. The original support act had pulled out, and it was a great feeling for us, because he asked for us personally – we were the only ones in the UK who he'd have doing the gig.

There were literally thousands of people there – the biggest crowd I'd ever played to. Of course, they were all there to see Eminem, but as the single had just gone to number one, everybody knew it, so we had all his fans shouting for us. That feeling alone will stay with me forever. Before we went on, we met Eminem. He's just a quiet kind of character, timid almost. Not scared – no way – but just not a loud person. You'll never hear him getting all excited – no 'Hey, man, how's it going, tell me what's happenin''. More like, 'Yeah … m-hm … cool …' He's a working man, and he'd been on the road for a long time, plus he meets a lot of people.

But it was good for me to meet him, not because I'm the sort of person to idolise guys like him, but simply because, for me, Eminem is one of the greatest, if not *the* greatest lyricist around today. To meet him was a real big moment in my life, something nobody can ever take away from me.

But I soon found out that there was to be a much more sinister side to my fame, too. I knew from growing up in south London what a dangerous place the street can be and, after my experiences as a kid being kidnapped and being stabbed, I guess the truth of the matter is that I began to get paranoid for my safety. But there's an old saying: just because you're paranoid, it doesn't mean they're not out to get you. And it soon transpired that somebody was, quite definitely, out to get me.

I'd written a lyric. Girls who don't make any money are called 'pigeons', and guys who are broke are called 'scrubs'. This lyric was about pigeons and scrubs, and I was using it on the radio. One day, somebody pointed out to me that some guy had taken my lyric, changed the structure of it around a bit, and was using it as his own. So I sent a shout out to this guy saying, 'Hey, man, don't use my lyrics. Use your own lyrics.'

This guy heard what I said and must have taken offence. He took it upon himself to wait outside my house in his car with a friend – and a gun. I arrived home and parked – I was with Natalie and Shayon at the time – and as I got out of the car he pulls up and calls my name: 'Asher!' I looked round to see him sitting in the passenger seat, pointing the gun at me.

He says to me that he's taken the lyric now, that it's his lyric. He gave me an ugly smile and said, 'What are you going to do about it?'

I shrugged. 'What do you think I'm going to do about it? You've got a gun pointed at me. Take the lyric, it's yours. I'll write another one.'

But that wasn't the end of it. Every time he saw me, he'd do

I got the gun because I feared for my life, my family's life and the life of my friends. I felt that if I had a gun I would be equal to anyone who comes to me to kill me – I would have as much chance of killing them, of defending myself.

basically the same thing, and as we lived in the same area, just up the street from each other, he saw me a lot.

Soon after that I started getting death threats on the phone. I don't know if it was from the same person, but, when you get a death threat, it doesn't really matter who it's from – it just scares you.

On another occasion I'm in my car just outside my house in Brixton and something smashes through the back windscreen. My immediate reaction is that it's gunshot, so I duck, and then one by one all my windows get smashed in. It's boys throwing bricks into my car. They all start running off and, thinking the coast is clear, I get out of my car. But then one of them stops and looks back. I see

With two fans.

Despite everything, there's no hard feelings towards traffic wardens!

that he has a gun in his hand and he's shouting, 'Come on, let's finish him, let's kill him!'

He starts coming back to get me, but his friends carry on running away. When he saw that they weren't coming back to help him he must have got scared and started running with them. I'd had a second lucky escape …

These experiences were becoming more and more common as I became more and more well known. I don't know why, but it seemed that certain people resented my success and, as their threats became more and more vicious, I became more and more paranoid. I figured that, one day, they were going to get me when there weren't that many people around, and I thought, I'm not taking that chance, man.

So I took it upon myself to make some calls and try and find out where I could get me a gun. Eventually I found this guy who could get me what I wanted, and I went to meet him.

The weapon he sold me was a pistol – just an ordinary starting pistol that you can buy in any sports shop, but it had been converted. I paid £1,300 for it. After I got arrested, I told the police how much it cost and they started laughing at me. It seems I'd been well and truly ripped off, but at the time I didn't care. You have to remember that I got the gun because I feared for my life, my family's life and the life of my friends. I felt that if I had a gun I would be equal to anyone who comes to me to kill me – I would have as much chance of killing them, of defending myself. It's weird, because I was so anxious to have the gun, but when it was in my possession I was terrified of it. I was shit scared in case it went off. I had it so that I could defend myself – the last thing I wanted was for it to cause anybody any harm.

The gun stayed in my possession for some time. Of course, I never had cause to use it, but somehow, although I was scared of it, it made me feel safer, made me feel that at least I could fight back now if I needed to. And the weapon stayed out of sight until July 30th 2001 – a day that I'll never forget as long as I live.

had an interview up in London's West End, so I drove into town with Natalie. I don't know what it was that made me take the gun with me – it was one of those days when you feel that nothing can happen to you, but I suppose those are the days that you're most likely to have something happen. After all, it took five minutes just to walk from my house to the car, and five minutes is a long time when you've been getting death threats.

So I went up west, did the interview and on the way back I said to Natalie that I needed to get something to drink. I pulled the car over into a parking bay, jumped out and went into a shop. When I got back, there was a traffic warden by the car and a parking ticket on the windscreen.

I started arguing with the warden. I said I'd only been there for two minutes, why did I have to pay? The warden said that the ticket was already in the system, and I just got more and more upset and started shouting at him. The traffic warden dug his heels in, and after a while I started laughing at him. I got back in the car, grabbed my bottle of water and put it through the sun roof, pretending to throw it at him.

At this point, another traffic warden came along – I think he was probably the guy who called the police. I drove off, and I got as far as Haymarket when all of a sudden these police cars are all over me. I pull over, and suddenly I'm surrounded by guns and everything. 'Hands on the wheel!' one of them shouts at me.

'What? What have I done?' I honestly couldn't see what I'd done

to warrant all this. They took me out of the car and said I'd pulled a gun on a traffic warden. 'What are you talking about?'

'You just pulled a gun on a traffic warden.'

'You're talking shit, brother. I never pulled a gun on nobody!'

'OK,' said the policeman, 'well, we're going to search you for a gun.'

My heart went into my mouth. I knew they'd find it, and sure enough, when they emptied Natalie's handbag, there it was. They found it straight away and hauled us in …

I was in the police station for two days. They questioned me for hour upon hour: how did I get the gun, why did I pull it on a traffic warden? I just told them the truth – including that I didn't pull it on the traffic warden – and eventually they let me out on bail. Ten thousand pounds.

I had to wait nine months for the case to come to trial. All that time I felt like a dagger was hanging over my head. I knew I didn't have any hope of being let off, but somewhere deep inside me I held on to the hope that the judge would be lenient on me given the circumstances that led me to have the gun in the first place. The thought of going to jail was too much for me to bear – the idea of not seeing my friends, not seeing my family, the kids. I tried to throw myself into my work, to concentrate on my art and try and make something positive out of the experience, but all the time I had the threat that I might be going to jail hanging over me.

Eventually I was sentenced. They threw out the charge of threatening the traffic warden with a gun. That was a relief to me, because I honestly hadn't done so, but I think it helped my case a bit that everybody hates traffic wardens! So all they could do me for was possession, and the judge took a pretty dim view of me carrying the weapon. Judge Geoffrey Rivlin sentenced me to 18 months in prison, and on that day I learned three important lessons: don't carry a gun, don't mess with traffic wardens and always pay your meters!

6

From 21 Seconds to 18 Months

SO I WENT TO JAIL – SENTENCED TO 18 MONTHS, SERVED NINE. I was at Feltham Young Offenders' Institute on remand for a month but, to be honest, I didn't really experience life there because I got segregated the minute I arrived. The screws had heard the inmates saying they were going to kill me as soon as I got there, so they took me away from the general prison population and so I never got an idea of what the place was really like – I couldn't go to the gym, I couldn't go to the church, I couldn't meet anyone new.

The weird thing was that I would sit in my cell and read stories in the newspaper where inmates were saying they'd beaten me up the day before – and I'd been in my cell all day and hadn't seen a single person. I read that I'd got a black eye, and I just thought, Shit, I'm glad I'm not me!

After a month I went to Rugby Young Offenders' Institute, which was much better for me as I was allowed into the general prison population. A lot of people there, including the prison staff, had

respect for me – I was even asked for autographs the day I arrived – so I knew as soon as I got there that things were going to be cool in that respect.

But that didn't mean that life was plain sailing. If you show any sign of weakness from the day you arrive, there are guys there who are going to make your life hell. You've got to be tough from day one. I went in there with a positive attitude. I was going to use my time well, to think about my responsibilities, and what I ought to be taking more seriously, and make sure that I never ended up in prison again.

For some people, it doesn't work like that; some people go into prison and come out just knowing more about crime. But I didn't want to learn about that stuff so, if I heard someone talking about crime, I'd just say, 'Fuck that, I don't want to learn about that. That's not me, I'm an artist, brother, do you get me? When I get out of here, I'm getting back to my life.' That was my attitude – I wasn't going to let prison change me, and people respected that.

I let it be known that I wasn't going to take any shit from anyone. There's big strapping guys in there, in the gym every day, pushing 100Ks on each side – they'd just have to flick me and I'd be knocked out. But even they knew I wasn't going to take it from anyone. Talk to me in the wrong way and I'm shouting at you. I'm going to give as good as I get and, even if you do beat me up, I know that next day you're not going to come back for more because you know I'm going to fight back. It's the most important lesson you learn – go to jail and get picked on, and that's what it's going to be like for the rest of your prison life, because people will see that you're weak.

My prison cell was tiny, maybe 10ft by 12ft, and that was for two people. There was a bunk bed, a TV up on the wall, a toilet, a basin and a table and chair each. That was it, all in that cramped space.

I worked in the prison kitchen, making the food. Life consisted of getting up, going to work for three hours, lunch, an hour's rest

I'm going to give as good as I get and even if you do beat me up, I know that next day you're not going to come back for more because you know I'm going to fight back. It's the most important lesson you learn – go to jail and get picked on, and that's what it's going to be like for the rest of your prison life, because people will see that you're weak.

and then back to work for another three hours. Then you'd have dinner, and be allowed a couple of hours' association – time to socialise, play pool, have a shower, make your phone calls, whatever. Then it's back to your cell for lock up, and the next day you do the same thing all over again. Your head gets locked into the same routine every day. That's just how life is. It's hard, especially when all you want to do is hug your kids and your girl. But you can't think like that. You've got to get your mind around the fact that you aren't going to see the ones you love, and so you end up thinking, Fuck everyone, fuck the world, fuck my girlfriend. It sounds harsh, but you have to do it, because, if you dwell on your situation, if you dwell on the fact that you're in prison and you're not going to see them, it'll eat you up inside. That's how suicide cases happen.

When you've got so much time to think, you overthink – What's she doing now, who's she with? When I was inside, my son broke his arm, and I just went nuts. The prison staff had to restrain me because I wouldn't calm down. I wanted to phone him, asap, just check he was allright, but it wasn't phone time, and I just had to deal with it.

I know that the stigma of having gone to prison will always be with me. When I was inside, I used to call my mum and say, 'Look at your boy, Mum, I'm famous, just like I always wanted to be.' She'd laugh because it was true, I always wanted to be famous, and I always wanted to be in the paper, but I never thought that it would take this to do it. Now I'm more infamous than famous. It's stupid

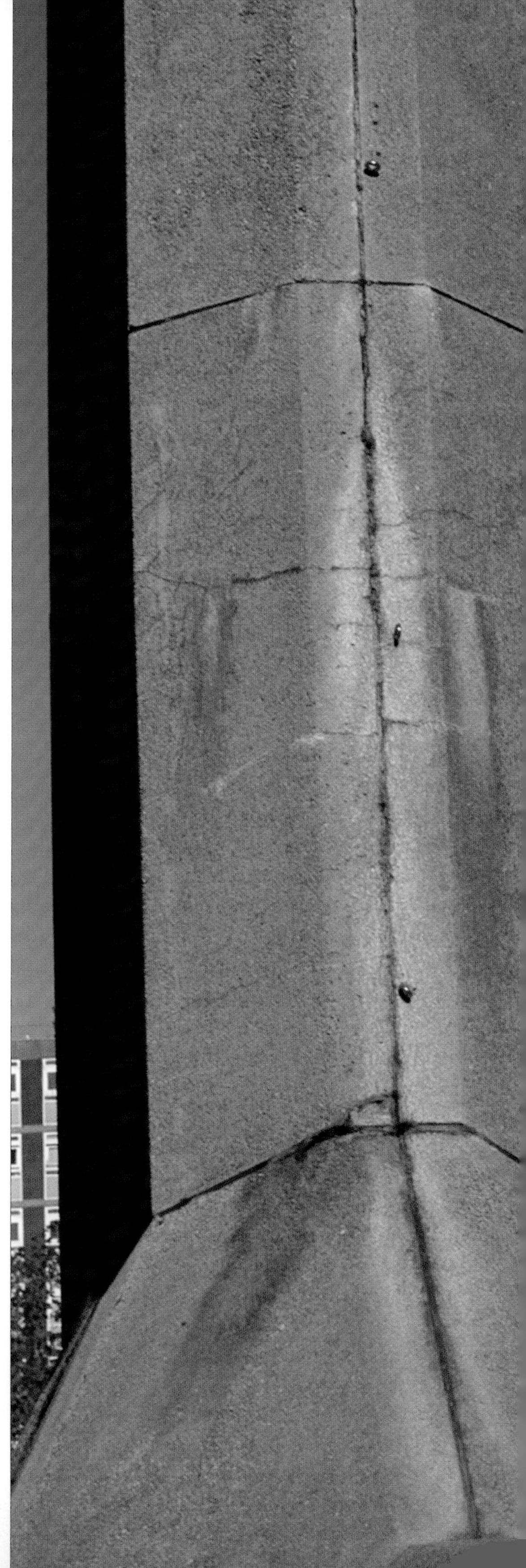

03

FREESTYLERS
03

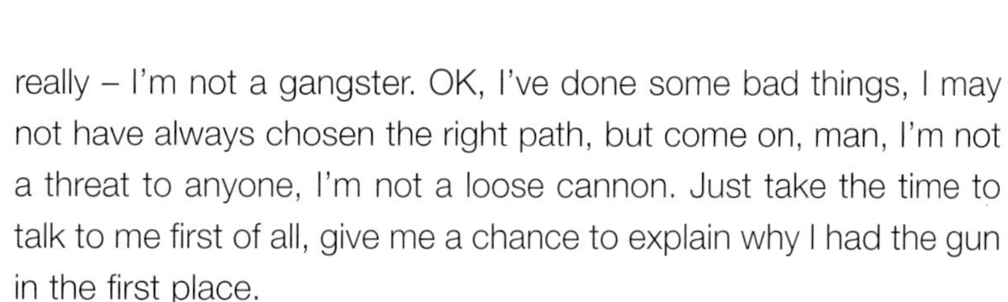

really – I'm not a gangster. OK, I've done some bad things, I may not have always chosen the right path, but come on, man, I'm not a threat to anyone, I'm not a loose cannon. Just take the time to talk to me first of all, give me a chance to explain why I had the gun in the first place.

But, once you've been to prison, you seldom get those chances. To most people it's just, Yeah, he had a gun, he killed people …

Prison gave me time to think about things, to sort my head out and also time to work on my lyrics. For me, inspiration for a lyric can come from anywhere, literally anywhere or anything. For me personally – and I know that a lot of other artists say this as well – I find that you can't just sit down and say, 'Yeah, I'm now going to write some lyrics.' You have to be inspired, something has to come over you. Michael Jackson says it's a gift from somewhere, a gift

With my mum.

from God. Well, I don't believe in God – I don't believe in any religion – so I have to get my inspiration elsewhere.

I've been through periods of three months when I couldn't write a word. I don't think that's necessarily a bad thing because, when you force yourself to sit down and write, it doesn't come out right, or at least it doesn't come out as well as if it came to you naturally.

That's how a lot of So Solid work. We're kind of spontaneous, we improvise a lot of the time, and that way we keep it real, keep it from the heart. I know that a lot of guys wouldn't agree with me, but the way I see it, if you practise too much, if you overperfect something, then you run the risk of it sounding stale. I'm more laid back about things, I go with the flow and see what comes

out. I don't put too much thought into it. I think that once you get to a certain level of ability, a certain standard, you can work like that. It's like at school, when you're writing essays and doing comprehension, practice makes perfect. At the beginning, when you start off, you can't do it that well, but you keep on practising and it starts to get easier.

I can go into the studio now and write lyrics in five minutes, and no one would know. Don't be fooled! Don't think a song's taken a week to make, I've just gone in there and done it. That's how we work. You ask some of these other artists, pop artists and the like, and they've been working on their album for years before they even deliver it to the record label. My last album took me a month, maybe two, to make, and I honestly believe that the more you focus and think about putting lyrics together, the harder it will be. Just roll with it. If something comes into your head, put it down on paper. Everything you write down could be the start of something else.

To people who are starting to write, who are where I was four or five years ago, I have this advice: just write about your daily life, write about your experience, but remember – keep it real. Only write about stuff that's happened to you.

So I used my time in prison to open my mind and let myself become a better lyricist. I also spent it preparing myself for the controversy I'd caused when I got out …

STL

7

The World According to Asher D

I KNEW THAT WHEN I WAS RELEASED I WAS GOING TO HAVE TO WORK HARD TO OVERCOME THE STIGMA THAT MY JAIL SENTENCE HAD GIVEN ME. All of a sudden, in the media's eyes, instead of being a serious performing artist, I'd become 'Asher D, member of So Solid Crew, jailed for gun crime'.

So Solid stood by me. They understood the situation I'd been in, and they knew that, just because we've got a dangerous image, it doesn't mean we're really dangerous people. Ask my girlfriend, she'll tell you. She'll say, 'Asher's a pussy!'

The trouble is that certain events have given us an image that we've found difficult to shake off. But the truth of the matter is that we've hardly had anything to do with events that have been pinned on us. I want to tell you about two controversial shows we've played, and then leave you to decide for yourself if what happened was down to the 'violent' So Solid Crew or not.

The first gig that we hit the headlines with was in Luton. It was a Delight FM rave, quite a long time ago now. For me, it was a perfect night – just a usual booking and everything went according to plan. I drove up there with a few people and arrived at the venue in good time. It's true that when I turned up I saw a few boys outside the club that I'd had some trouble with, and I remember thinking, Right, this is a bit hot, but I had a booking, it was my job, so I just got on with it.

When we were on stage, everything was neat – there were a few rowdy people in the club, but they weren't causing trouble, so everything was cool. The gig finished, and I went home.

It wasn't until the next day that I read in the papers that there had been some serious trouble outside. These two boys had some sort of confrontation – one of them was there by himself and the other had ten or 15 people with him. He was completely outnumbered and they rushed at him with weapons – knives, bats, whatever. He didn't stand a chance. I only know the details because when I was in jail I met people who knew the guy who got killed, so I heard little bits of the story; but on the actual night, I went home, went to sleep and woke up to read: MORE VIOLENCE AT SO SOLID GIG. I just thought, Wow, when I left it was nice, it was cool.

More recently was a show at London's Astoria, a really important gig for So Solid. Again, it was a Delight FM event, and it wasn't just us on the bill – we had other artists from the station booked to be there. I think that Pay As You Go and Heartless were meant to be around, but I don't know if they were because, as it turned out, the evening didn't go on that long.

Around that time was when we were having a lot of problems. A load of guns were coming into play on the streets, I was awaiting trial for my gun offence, people were harassing me because of the hype and whatever. We weren't exactly expecting trouble that night, but we went to the gig with a feeling that some sort of shit might be going down. We had a lot of security with us, because we had this feeling that it might be touch and go …

'For years I've been worried about the hateful lyrics that these boasting, macho idiots come out with, from these rappers and so on. It is a big cultural problem.'

Culture Minister Kim Howells

We sat in the dressing room for hours, as we'd got there ages before the gig was supposed to start. Eventually the call came for us to go on. There were 30 or 40 of us all going down the stairs to go on to the stage, and by this time I was probably half-drunk already, so my senses weren't really aware of everything!

We got on stage, and I'm there in the middle of it all, doing my thing, and I notice this commotion going on to the left of me. I think maybe someone on the stage had knocked their drink and it splashed on someone in the audience. The people in the audience retaliated by throwing drink back, and all of a sudden, from nowhere, two boys rushed the stage. Somehow everyone else took that as a lead to follow. Suddenly two of the boys on stage – I don't know why, whether they were from different areas or something – started having a big argument, and before I knew it a couple of people had pulled guns. It was coming to the point where someone could easily have got shot.

Security went mad. It's their job to protect us, and they don't know who these people are on stage, or why they're there, so they tried to get us off as quickly as possible. They formed a barrier around the whole Crew, rushed us off stage and shouted at us to make our way back down to the dressing room. But there were so many of us, and everyone was so confused, that we started going down this flight of stairs – the dressing rooms were upstairs – and there's this whole commotion, girls screaming and everything. We were heading towards the back door, and as we got there security opened it and me, Swiss, Mac,

Face and Dan all spilled out the door as we were in the front of the crowd.

As we got outside I remember looking round and seeing these boys – I don't know how many, but a decent number – all with weapons. They spot us, shout, 'There they are,' and start chasing us. We looked behind us, and the doors had been closed, so we just ran out into Tottenham Court Road with these guys hot on our heels. Somehow we managed to lose them, and eventually we got to some block of flats – I don't know where it was – and we just crouched by a wall in silence. One of us had the number of a car firm, so we called them up on the mobile and they came and collected us.

Again, it wasn't until I'd gone home, gone to sleep and woken up the next morning that I read the newspaper and saw that some guy had got shot at the Astoria. I saw the guns, but I didn't see them getting used. But that was the controversy – that was what we were supposed to have started, and in the eyes of the media, and eventually even the government, that was our fault. The truth of the matter was that it was just our gig. We'd come to do a booking and someone spoiled it. That's what happens the majority of the time …

It's stuff like this that has led all sorts of people to misinterpret what So Solid Crew are all about. They say that So Solid glorifies gun culture and violence, but they don't understand that it's quite the other way round. We've grown up on the street, and we've seen what's happening out there, and what we're rapping about is just a reflection of what's going on.

Music and crime, man, they are not related. Any idiot can tell you that, they are not brother and sister. Anybody who says they are is talking bullshit. I'd be quite happy to take any politician who thinks that way to spend a day with me on the street, and I'd show them where the real problem lies. I'd show them the guys going through dustbins looking for food. I'd show them the junkies trying to buy

crack on the corner. I'd show them the dealers on the front line in Brixton, five bags of weed in their hands and the police walking by not giving a shit. It's all there to be seen with your own eyes, and the truth is that the politicians don't need me to show it to them – they know it's happening, and they just don't want to deal with it.

They know Brixton is a ghetto. Everyone knows it is, it's common knowledge, but I think that's how the government wants it to be. They don't want the people living in Peckham to be living in the West End – it's going to ruin the West End for them! They don't want the people who live in Brixton to live in Chelsea. So where are they going to put them? It's no coincidence that it's all Africans, Jamaicans and Somalians living in the North Peckham Estate. Why do all the Kosovans live in Brixton? Someone's putting them there.

So what's happening is that all the poor people are being put in the same place together, and it's the poverty that's breeding the crime and the addictions. I read that 30 per cent of the crack that comes into this country comes via couriers from Jamaica. And I'm thinking, Who's bringing in the rest? Personally, I don't know any black people who own boats or planes – no one who can bring in that amount of crack cocaine without getting caught. What about the guns? Where are all these Uzis coming from, because they're not made here. They're made in America and, let me tell you, I can't take ten machine guns in a plane with me and not get noticed. Someone's bringing them in, there's an arms trade and a drugs trade, and it's not being run by poor ethnic minorities in a south London ghetto.

I swear to God the black population is dying out. We're killing each other on the streets, man, over drugs and money and it's an everyday occurrence. There's a guy I knew at school, we were friends when we were very young, and he's a dealer now. He's been having a lot of trouble in the Peckham area and, whenever he sees this particular Peckham dealer, they have a shoot-up. You walk around my area and there's always these yellow police incident signs up, and it's always him. He rings me up and says, 'Ash, you see that new sign, that's me,' and he's proud of it. It's everyday life for him, he walks out of his house, he's sees this other guy in a fast food joint and they start shooting at each other. This isn't how it's meant to be, but this is what the street is coming to because people in high places aren't doing anything about it.

If politicians wanted to stop the problem, they would. They could stop creating the ghettos, they could stop being involved in the arms trade, but they're just not willing to get involved. It's much easier for them to wipe their hands of it by finding a scapegoat – blame it on So Solid! Ashley's just come out of jail for having a loaded weapon, blame the whole problem on that. And the more you pin it all on us, the more it's going to look like we're involved.

The truth is, hundreds of thousands of people listen to So Solid's

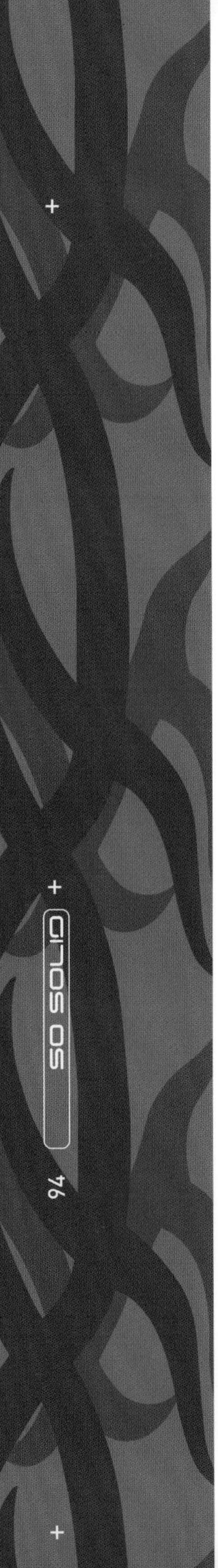

music, and don't go around shooting people. The people who buy our records, the fans, they don't misinterpret what we're saying. They know that acts of violence are down to an individual. Show me one person who's going to listen to a piece of music, pick up a gun and say, 'Yeah, I'm gonna go and kill someone now.' It just doesn't happen that way. That's not reality. Individuals who do this shit have problems – whether they're mental problems or social problems or whatever, and to blame them on music is just covering the problem up.

And if the music of So Solid Crew is promoting violence, then so are all sorts of other things. Some expert on TV with a 9mm gun saying, 'This is how you load it' – ban him! He's promoting violence! *Pulp Fiction*? Ban it! It's promoting violence! All those films with guns? Ban them! They're promoting violence! All those old American country singers sing about guns and killing people – do the government blame them? Of course not – they're not an easy target, not an easy scapegoat.

If they carry on with their heads in the sand, things are only going to get worse. If they think it's bad now, what do they think it's gonna be like when the shit really hits the fan and it becomes like America? I'm OK – I'm black. It's not going to be me they come after when they want some serious money – it's the big businesses, the real rich people who are going to be told, 'Give me your money, or you're dead.' It's only going to get worse, when street crime starts becoming intelligent and real, and only the people in office have the power to stop it happening.

The politicians who blame us for their social problems have got to stop being hypocrites. Hundreds of thousands of people campaign against a war that they don't want to be waged, and what do the government do? They go to war. The minute they disagree with someone, they go and shoot them up. What kind of example do they think that sets? How do they think that actions like that help prevent gun culture, how is that going to prevent violence on the streets? They need to start dealing with the real issues: they

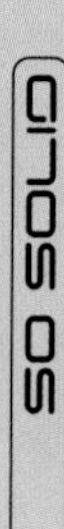
SO SOLID

need to see that the state we're in derives from social deprivation, from their own social policies, from the way ethnic minorities are treated. They've got to understand that it all comes from the poverty in the ghettos they've created, where people are forced into crime and drugs because they've got no other way out …

It's the kids we've got to focus on, the kids coming up. The people out there on the streets, selling crack and doing it themselves – they're a lost cause. They'll die or end up in jail. But the kids who are in school now, we've got to get their minds set, make them realise that they've got to do something with their lives, give them options. You can't just take someone who's thinking of becoming a drug dealer and say, 'Here's a job in a fast food joint for four pounds an hour.' They'll just say, 'What? I can earn ten grand a day selling my drugs, what are you, stupid?' You've got to give them an alternative, give them a job that's going to pay them a decent wage that they can survive on – not £100 benefit when they've got two kids.

People need social promises, they need a little excitement and they need to know that they've got a chance out there to make something of their lives. That's the whole ethos behind what So Solid Crew want to achieve. We're going through all the badness, the experience of the press hating us and the humiliation of going to jail and whatever to break the barriers for kids coming up. In five or ten years' time, black music will be regular, like pop. We want to change the way young people think about their future so they don't look at the crackheads on the street and think that's the only path open to them – they look at So Solid and think, Yeah, it's possible for ethnic minorities to achieve something worthwhile.

It's the same thing with me going to jail. In a way, it's a Jesus thing – they say Jesus died for us and, in the same way, I'm going through what I'm going through so that other people, young people coming up, don't have to. And I know that it's getting through to people, because I get a lot of love and respect. The other day I went to the supermarket and I got to the counter and this woman sees me and starts crying. 'Oh my God, you're Asher D!' She starts hugging me. 'I'm so glad you're out of jail, back in your home. Be good, man, take care, we love you!' She was like my mum. So I know that we've had an impact on the black community – we're hope for them, they see us as guys who have broken barriers, gone to another world. I used to get ten fan mails a day, girls saying how they tried to commit suicide when they heard I was going to jail, but they're having counselling now. It's a huge responsibility, but I think that the people who matter realise that, far from trying to glorify the terrifying gun culture on the streets of Britain today, we're really just trying to help …

So, when people turn up to our gigs and cause trouble that gets reflected on us, it upsets me, makes me feel hurt. Because they don't understand that what So Solid are doing is not just to better ourselves, but to better everyone, every black person out there, every ethnic minority that doesn't have the same chance as us. In all those little communities where people are poor and struggling, all these urban areas, you've got kids with talent – talent at music, or sport, or whatever. Our aim, So Solid as a whole, when we've conquered it all, is to let those kids in, give them a chance to make changes in their lives, in their children's lives, and by extension in the lives of everyone. It's a chain reaction, and these people putting us down, spoiling our raves with fighting or shooting, are spoiling it for everyone. It's just stupid. It stops us moving forwards.

And moving forwards is what it's all about. I'm a young man, and I've got more experience behind me than most people twice my age, but if people think I'm gonna take a step back, if people think that I'm gonna let the shit that gets said about me ruin the plans I have for the future, well, then, they've got another thing coming …

8

The Future

WHEN I CAME OUT OF PRISON, I SAID TO MYSELF, 'RIGHT, THAT'S IT! A COUPLE OF YEARS' TIME, DUDE, I'M GONNA BE ALLRIGHT!' It was time to make some major league moves, to take things to a different level. I've been in this business for years, I've had a lot of success, but the time had come for me to make sure that my kids had the lifestyle I never had, that my family had a chance.

For me, going to jail was high drama. I'd think to myself, What's going to happen when I get out of this cell? This could be the end. So I knew the time had come for me to start hustling. A lot of people, they just lie on their back and say, 'Wouldn't it be good if I did this or that.' Well, that ain't me. When I decide on something, I go for it, and when I was released I decided that I was going to make sure that the future happens for me.

For me, the future lies in America. Land of opportunity! It always surprises me when people decide they want to come over to this

country in order to get away. In terms of the music that I make, there's so much more to be made in America. Over here, the main thing is pop, and not that many people are into the kind of music that I create. In America, everything is taken far more seriously.

Over there, if you're shit, you're shit, and they'll let you know. It's very rare to find a bad singer with a record deal, because they've got so many talented artists out there. So, while it might look to us as though, wow, everyone can sing in America, the truth is that they only pick the very best.

In the UK, you can get on *Top of the Pops* just because you look good. They put you in some expensive clothes, plaster you in make-up, and that's good enough to sell that product, regardless of whether you're a good singer or not. Over in America, that shit just doesn't work. The whole scene is just much more real.

BRIXTO
VARIE
6 MARKET ROW
JUDO

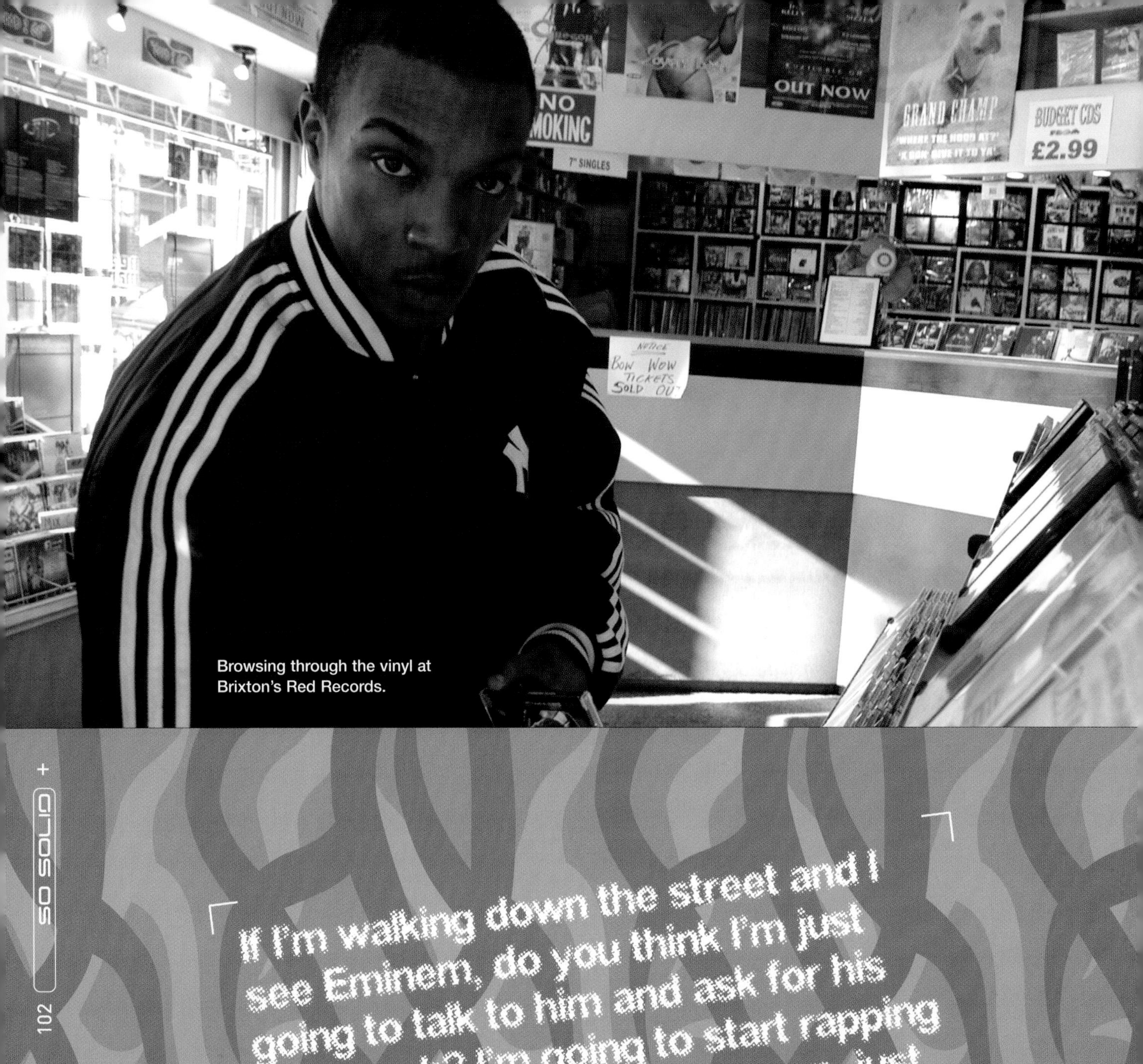

Browsing through the vinyl at Brixton's Red Records.

If I'm walking down the street and I see Eminem, do you think I'm just going to talk to him and ask for his autograph? I'm going to start rapping at him, seriously, for no reason, just so he knows who I am.

And obviously, of course, hip hop started in the States. We're still having to go through what those artists went through all those years ago: the police wanted to shut it down, the government didn't like it. The same thing's happening over here with urban music, and we're just going to have to fight till we get it to that same level that black musicians managed to do in America. Even when we manage it though, even when we get the door open, break that barrier, the bottom line is there's still only a certain number of units to be sold in England. England's this little place, and America's that many times bigger, so it's a natural progression for artists who really want to make an impression ...

When I come out of this game, I want to be financially stable for the rest of my life. I have to be. The idea scares me, but I know I've got no other choice. I simply can't see myself going back to college to learn a new trade, or working a nine-to-five desk job. It's not me. I've got big ambitions and I want big things to happen – for that, I want big money, David Beckham money! So it's only natural that I set my sights on America.

One day soon, I'm going to pack my bags, take my album and a few other tunes that I've done, and just go. Book a flight and just go, man. I'll study a few addresses first, see where all the important labels are, and then just go and push myself on as many people as I can, flood my music out there. I'll work with as many people as possible, get a rapport going, and then just make my music. I've got the gift of the gab, I can talk my way into anywhere. Most people don't dare to do it, to just put yourself in the front line, but I know that, if you just go over there and show off, it can work for you! So if I'm walking down the street and I see Eminem, do you think I'm just going to talk to him and ask for his autograph? I'm going to start rapping at him, seriously, for no reason, just so he knows who I am. And he'll go away thinking about me – even if he thinks I'm shit, he'll still be thinking about me: 'Hey, that guy just came up and started rapping at me from nowhere!'

That's my thing – I'm brave enough to put my arse on the line and just do it, because that's the only way you can get what you want. You can't be scared of what anyone's going to think, or what anyone's going to say about you, because that way you never do anything. You've just got to cut through it. Think about it – we can do anything we want to do. Look at Rockerfeller Records. They started out with nothing, and look what they've got now. They just made moves, man. Jay-Z sells clothes. He makes more money selling clothes than he does selling records. He makes hundreds of millions a year and he came from the equivalent of a housing estate in Peckham. That stuff can happen for you in America, and that's why it's the next step for me.

I'm lucky. Unlike a lot of people, I've got other strings to my bow – especially acting. Performing is in my blood and the acting is another side of it to the music. I love to act. Funny thing is, when I'm doing it, I don't really think about what I'm doing. Maybe that's what makes a good actor – someone who can be natural on screen and just do something the way they would if it was really happening. A lot of people come up to me, journalists and people, and say, 'Hey, Asher, you're critically acclaimed for your acting,' and I feel as surprised as they are. I wonder, What is it I do that's so good?!

I speak to a lot of good writers and directors, and I get film offers a lot. The problem is that a lot of the films are the same, the same stereotype. Before I went to jail, I'd probably get asked to play a drug dealer, or someone typical of a young black man, but I didn't want to get typecast. I didn't want to get stuck in the kind of role where, if I'd done it, and done it well, everyone would want me to do the same role in their film too. That's why I stayed away from soaps – I had an offer to be in *EastEnders*, but again I didn't want to find myself in a role that I couldn't get out of.

After I came out of jail, everyone wanted me to do something with a gun. I see a lot of really good scripts, and if I think that the direction of the film is to expose the situation that exists out there,

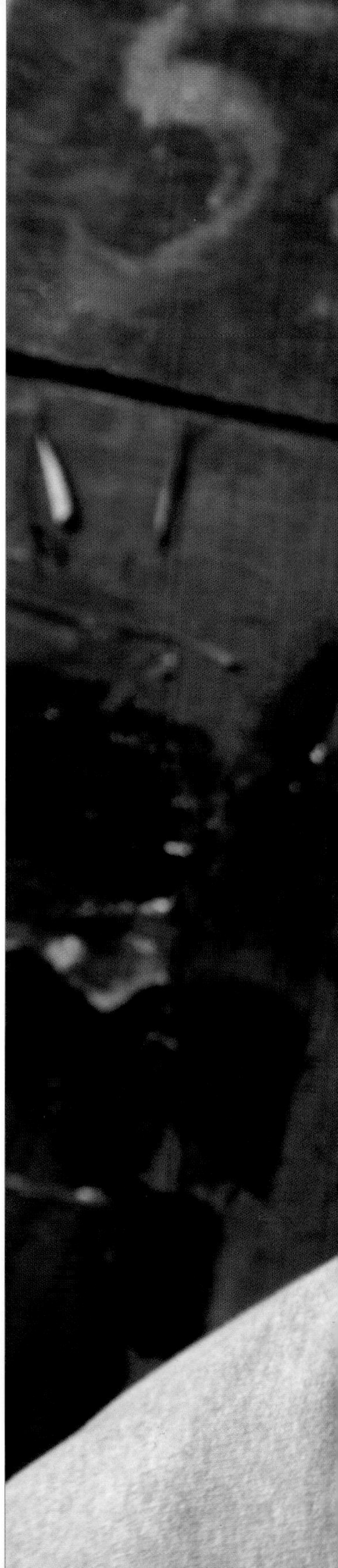

to do a good piece of work that is going to tell a story about what is going on in the inner city or whatever, then that's good; but if it's an out-and-out stereotype and it's got no meaning to it then I'm not interested. The key lies in trying to pick the right ones.

I've got an exciting project coming up. It's called *The Boys* and it's a feature film that tells the truth about gun culture at the moment. It's very cutting edge, and I think it has its finger right on the pulse of what's happening in the streets at the moment. It's going to be filmed like a documentary, and most of the dialogue is going to be improvised. It's all very exciting.

Other than that I've a few more deals on the table at the moment. I'm doing a film called *House of Nine*. It's a horror movie, also starring Dennis Hopper. It should be good and lead to other big things for me.

So the future is looking good, looking bright. I'm completely focused now on trying to carry on making a success of my life, and at the same time not to let fame go to my head – to keep my feet on the ground. I meet a lot of famous people on a daily basis, just people in the industry, and, to me, they're just normal guys. I don't believe the hype. I go to the supermarket and see Simon from Blue – one time I bumped into him in the supermarket and I'd just heard they'd signed a multi-million-pound promotional deal, and I'm like, 'What are you doing here, you're a multi-millionaire.'

He tells me, 'Asher, I'm a human being, I've got to eat!' And it's true, man, we've all got to eat. You can only live within your means, and I don't have any time for people with money and attitude. I don't spend my time around people like that – in fact, I try not to be in places where I know every celebrity is going to be. I don't like people who think that they are above everyone else – they can't integrate with normal people any more. They've forgotten how to talk. I don't want to lose that, and that's why I have to hug the street a bit. I'm always going to be connected to the street, no matter how much money I make.

I just want to do the best I can – not just for me but for the whole of So Solid Crew. That's the way we work. There's rivalry about all our different solo careers, but it's good-natured rivalry. We're all part of the Crew so, if someone else wins, we all win. It doesn't matter if somebody else does better than you, because it all helps So Solid. Together, we want to make a difference. That's why we're getting heavily involved in our anti-gun campaigning.

My anti-gun views have always been my opinion, regardless of whether I had the gun and went to jail. I've never thought guns are good, I've never been excited by picking up a gun. Whenever I picked it up, it was out of desperation, out of me thinking, I'm going to die today. I think it's only right that I explain to people why I did what I did. I know what I did was wrong, and if, from being in my position, I can use my name to promote a good cause, then it's only right that I should do it. If I'm playing at a club

and people are going to listen to me at an anti-gun seminar beforehand, that's good. If I can show people who were in the same position what happened to me, then maybe it can stop them going down the same path. I can relate to it better than anyone else, better than Tony Blair – he doesn't even know what a Glock feels like!

I still get the same harassment, the same people are still after me, the street is still just as dangerous a place, but I'm living without the gun. I'm getting through without it and, if I can do that, then so can anyone else in that situation.

I'm legit now – that's it. And I feel better for it. If someone wants to take my life, I'll just have to be ready to face my fear. And if that person kills me, that was my time. That was my life, and I'll know that I've done with it everything that I could have.